Zodiac
Felties

16 compelling astrological characters to craft

Nicola Tedman & Sarah Skeate

Andrews McMeel
Publishing, LLC

Kansas City • Sydney • London

Andrews McMeel Publishing, LLC
an Andrews McMeel Universal company
1130 Walnut Street, Kansas City, Missouri 64106
www.andrewsmcmeel.com

ISBN: 978-1-4494-1168-8

Library of Congress Control Number: 2011932651

This book was conceived,
designed, and produced by
Ivy Press
210 High Street
Lewes
East Sussex BN7 2NS
United Kingdom
www.ivy-group.co.uk

Creative Director Peter Bridgewater
Publisher Sophie Collins
Editorial Director Tom Kitch
Senior Designer James Lawrence
Designer Kevin Knight
Photographer Andrew Perris
Illustrator Melvyn Evans

Printed in China

Color origination by
Ivy Press Reprographics

12 13 14 15 16 IYP 10 9 8 7 6 5 4 3 2 1

Attention: Schools and Businesses
Andrews McMeel books are available at quantity discounts with bulk purchase for educational, business, or sales promotional use. For information, please e-mail the Andrews McMeel Publishing Special Sales Department: specialsales@amuniversal.com

Important
Safety warning: The felties are not toys. All the figures are small and many have removable parts, making them a choking hazard. They are not suitable for children under the age of three.

Contents

A design for a pop-up card that can be scanned or copied and used to present a birthday feltie to a lucky recipient, or simply as a home for your own felties to rest in when you're not consulting them on your astrological future.

Starting Out

How to make a feltie worthy of its place in the zodiac

You'll want all your creations to hit the heights of the cosmos, so be sure to read these few pages before you make a start. We'll describe the stitches you need to use and the clever techniques that will make all the difference to your finished figures. Don't give your felties to the kids, however—many have small or sharp pieces, so they don't make suitable playthings.

Tools

Use a sharp pair of scissors for cutting and snipping, and the smallest embroidery needle you're happy with to add stitched details and to sew the felties together. A few characters specify use of eyelet pliers. These are inexpensive and available online or from craft stores—just follow the manufacturer's directions for your model.

The felties call for two kinds of glue: rubber cement and superglue. The best way to use rubber cement is to spread a thin layer over both the surfaces to be stuck together, wait for a few seconds so that the glue becomes more tacky, then press the glued surfaces together. For very small areas, use a matchstick or a toothpick to help you spread the glue thinly. Superglue is very strong and fast acting; the main thing to be careful about is to avoid inadvertently adhering together items that you didn't mean to.

A nonpermanent fabric marker (again easily available) is used on many of the felties to draw lines on the fabric that disappear after a few days. Use it to mark out stitching or details.

Templates

Scan or photocopy the pattern pieces from the printed page at 100 percent, then simply cut them out. If you don't have access to a scanner and printer or photocopier, trace the pattern pieces for the character you want to make onto tracing paper with a soft pencil. All the templates in the book are the correct size to make the zodiac felties shown; none needs scaling up or down.

Stuffing the Felties

Use a loose polyester stuffing to fill your felties. It's light and easy to separate into wisps for stuffing the dolls. Don't be tempted to use cotton balls or batting instead—they'll clump and make for a less-than-starry result. A matchstick or pointed tweezers will help you to distribute the stuffing evenly in the smallest pieces.

Sewing and Embroidery

All the characters are embroidered and sewn together using embroidery floss. This comes in a small skein with thread made up of six separate strands, and you pull the floss apart to get the number of strands specified in the patterns. It's mostly used in single or double threads, although in a few cases more strands are needed. To get the number of strands you want, cut a short length of floss, around 12 to 16 in. (30 to 40 cm) long, and gently separate the number of strands required from the main piece, pulling gently from one end. Keep the other strands to use later. To secure the thread, either tie a small knot at the end of the floss, or make a tiny cross-stitch (one strand laid over another). Whichever method you choose, start from the wrong side of the felt piece. All the patterns specify using an embroidery needle unless you are sewing on beads, in which case use a beading needle. This has a very narrow head so that the beads slip over it easily.

If you aren't used to embroidering, practice on a scrap of felt before working on your zodiac felties. None of the stitches described is difficult, but one or two—French knots in particular—can take some practice to get perfect.

The Stitches

Overhand Stitch

The overhand stitch is used to attach two pieces of fabric together. This isn't a decorative stitch, so always use thread that matches the color of the felt, and keep the stitches small and neat.

1 Take a strand of embroidery floss and align the two pieces of fabric to be sewn together. Bring the thread through from the wrong side of one of the pieces and make a small stitch at right angles to the edges of both felt pieces, going over both edges and taking the needle through both layers of felt.

2 Push the needle back through the felt, bringing it out a little farther along from where you started, and make a second stitch over the edges of both pieces of felt.

Backstitch

This stitch makes a plain unbroken line.

1 Thread the needle with one or two strands of floss, as directed, then bring it up through the fabric at the point at which you want the line of stitching to start.

2 Make a stitch going in the opposite direction to the way you want your backstitch line to continue, and bring the needle back up through the fabric one stitch's length away in the direction in which you want the stitching line to go.

3 Take the thread backward and push the needle through the point at which the first stitch finished. Bring it out one stitch's length in front of the thread. Continue until the length of your line of backstitch is complete. Fasten off.

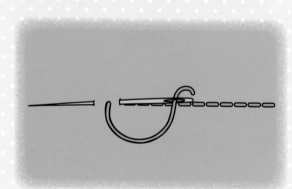

Satin Stitch

This stitch is used for filling small areas solidly.

To cover small areas, make a series of single parallel stitches close to one another, creating a solid area of threads. Satin stitch is usually worked neatly with stitches running exactly parallel, but in some cases—for instance, where an area to be filled in with color is an irregular shape—you can work stitches that overlap slightly or are placed at a slight angle to one another. If these stitches are made neatly, the effect of solid color will still be achieved.

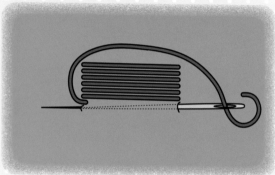

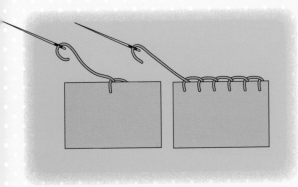

Blanket Stitch

Blanket stitch can be used along the edge of a piece or pieces of fabric, either decoratively or to join two pieces together. It leaves an "edging" of thread along its outer edge.

1 Bring the needle up through the fabric (or through both pieces if you are joining fabric) a little way in from the edge (the length that you want your stitch to be).

2 Hook the thread around the point of the needle and pull the needle directly up through the fabric. The thread will be held along the edge of the fabric by the stitch. Insert the needle back through the fabric to start the next stitch.

French Knot

This stitch makes a small, decorative knot that stands above the surface of the felt.

1 Thread a needle with the number of strands specified in the instructions, fasten the end on the wrong side of the felt, and bring the needle out on the right side where you want to make your French knot. Use your left thumb to hold the thread down at the point at which it emerges from the felt, and wrap the thread twice around the needle.

2 Keep your thumb in place on the felt and bring the needle back through the felt very close to where it emerged (not in exactly the same spot, however, or the thread will simply be pulled back through the hole).

3 Push the needle through to the back of the felt and pull the thread taut. A small textured knot will be left on the right side of the felt. Fasten off the thread on the wrong side, or go on to make your next French knot.

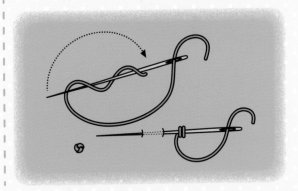

Baseball Stitch

Baseball stitch is used to join two edges that abut one another. Those zodiac felties with cone-shaped or cylindrical bodies can be closed up using this stitch.

1 Bring a needle up through one piece of fabric a little way in from the edge (the length that you want your stitch to be).

2 Take it down through the space between the two pieces of fabric that you are joining, and bring it up through the back of the other edge, one stitch length in.

3 Repeat, taking the needle between the space and up through the other piece of fabric, to create a row of stitches running alternately between the two pieces of fabric.

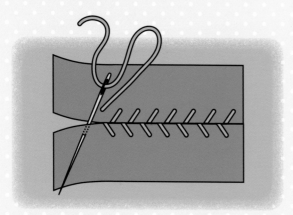

Beading

Use a beading needle to add beads and sequins. Beads are sewn on by bringing the needle through from the back of the felt, threading the bead onto the needle, then pushing the needle back through the fabric near where it first emerged and pulling the thread tight.

To add a sequin, bring the needle up through the felt, thread on the sequin, and secure it by taking a stitch over to the edge on each side (or use more stitches to make a decorative star shape on top of your sequin). Alternatively, you can use a bead to secure the sequin in the center (see the instructions opposite).

To Secure a Sequin with a Bead

1 Thread a needle and bring it up through the felt to the right side. Thread the sequin and then the bead onto the needle.

2 Take the needle back through the centered hole in the sequin, pull the thread tight, and fasten off securely at the back of the felt. The bead, being larger than the centered hole in the sequin, will hold the sequin in place.

3 To add more beads, make a short stitch to the next point and add the next bead. Repeat, knotting after each one, and then fasten off securely at the back.

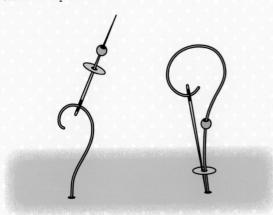

Tips

- The felties are marked with stars indicating the degree of difficulty—the simplest with a single star, the hardest with three or four. None is very difficult, but it's best to start with one of the easier models before tackling a four-star constellation.

- Pick one of the brightest or darkest felties for your first project—when you're starting out, you'll be more likely to handle the felt more and the paler colors can become grubby.

- Because felt doesn't fray, it's ideal for working at this scale, but if a pattern piece is really tiny, apply an extremely thin layer of rubber cement over the wrong side of the fabric and let it dry before you cut the pieces out. This stiffens the felt a little, and the cut pieces will have sharp edges.

March 21–April 20 • Ruled by *Mars* • Element *Fire* • Color *Red* • Gemstone *Diamond*

Aries the Ram

DIFFICULTY RATING

Dancing on a volcano is the Ram's idea of a good time. Risk, fire, likelihood of certain death, plus the possibility of adrenalin-soaked last-minute escape: Welcome to Aries heaven. Stitch your Ram with panache, and don't worry too much about neatening the edges—rams are big on creativity, not nit-picking.

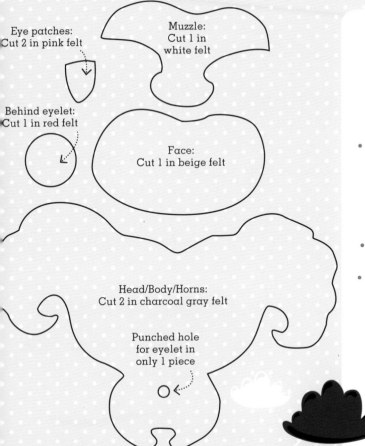

Eye patches:
Cut 2 in pink felt

Muzzle:
Cut 1 in
white felt

Behind eyelet:
Cut 1 in red felt

Face:
Cut 1 in beige felt

Head/Body/Horns:
Cut 2 in charcoal gray felt

Punched hole
for eyelet in
only 1 piece

YOU WILL NEED

- 6-in. (15-cm) square of charcoal gray felt
- 3-in. (7.5-cm) square of white felt
- 2-in. (5-cm) square of beige felt
- Small scraps of red and pink felt
- Embroidery floss in white, beige, bright pink, red, and dark gray
- 1 white snowflake-shaped sequin
- 1 bronze-colored eyelet, ⅛ in. (3 mm) diameter
- 2 white sequins
- 1 bronze heart-shaped pendant charm, approx. ⁵⁄₁₆ in. (8 mm) long
- Tiny quantity of loose polyester stuffing
- Pencil and tracing paper
- Nonpermanent fabric marker
- Scissors
- Eyelet pliers
- Rubber cement
- Embroidery needle
- Matchstick or tweezers

To make *Aries*

1 Cut out all the felt pieces as marked, either photocopying or scanning the templates, or using tracing paper to make templates, as described on page 4. Use the eyelet pliers to punch a hole in the center of Aries's stomach, as marked on the pattern piece, and through the center of the snowflake sequin. Again using the eyelet pliers, fasten the bronze eyelet through the snowflake and the front of the body piece. Use rubber cement to attach the red circle on the back of the front body piece so that you see red through the eyelet hole.

2 Using rubber cement, glue the muzzle onto the face piece, then position the eye patches and glue them in place (use the photograph of the finished feltie for reference). Adhere the face in place on the front of the body, above the snowflake.

3 Thread a needle with a single strand of white embroidery floss and sew around the edge of the muzzle with a small overhand stitch. Rethread the needle with a single strand of beige thread and use a small overhand stitch to sew around the lower edge of the face, through the body.

4 Thread a needle with two strands of bright pink embroidery floss and sew three single stitches on Aries's muzzle to make his nose. Go over each stitch a second time to emphasis the shape, then fasten off the thread on the wrong side of the felt.

5 Thread a needle with two strands of red floss and sew the white sequins in place on the eye patches, using two stitches, one over the other.

6 Thread a needle with two strands of white floss and sew the bronze heart charm in the center of Aries's forehead.

7 Align the front and back body pieces, right sides out. Thread a needle with one strand of dark gray floss and sew the body parts together with a small overhand stitch. Start at the outer edge of the right horn and sew around the body to the same point on the left horn as shown. Stuff the body carefully with small wisps of the stuffing using a matchstick or tweezers to help you. When it is firm, but not too tightly packed, sew the gap across the top of the head closed.

8 Thread a needle with two strands of beige floss and sew single stitches at the bottom of each leg to make the hooves. Fasten the thread off neatly inside the body.

April 21–May 21 • Ruled by *Venus* • Element *Earth* • Colors *Pink & pale blue* • Gemstone *Emerald*

Taurus the Bull

The Bull believes in quality, and plenty of it. So use top-notch materials and your best stitches, or your Bull may charge, tear the needle from your incompetent hand, and finish the job himself.

YOU WILL NEED

- 6-in. (15-cm) square of sage green felt
- 4-in. (10-cm) square of pink felt
- 2-in. (5-cm) square of cream felt
- Tiny scrap of flesh pink felt
- Embroidery floss in cream, pink, and sage green
- 2 turquoise eyelets, ⅛ in. (3 mm) diameter
- 1 bronze metallic ring from a toggle fastening, ⅝ in. (15 mm) diameter
- 2 miniature black paper fasteners
- 1-ft. (30-cm) length of light blue organza ribbon, ⅛ in. (3 mm) wide
- 1 small flower-shaped mother-of-pearl button
- Tiny quantity of loose polyester stuffing
- Pencil and tracing paper
- Nonpermanent fabric marker
- Scissors
- Eyelet pliers
- Metal snips
- Round needle-nose pliers
- Awl
- Pins
- Embroidery needle
- Rubber cement
- Matchstick or tweezers

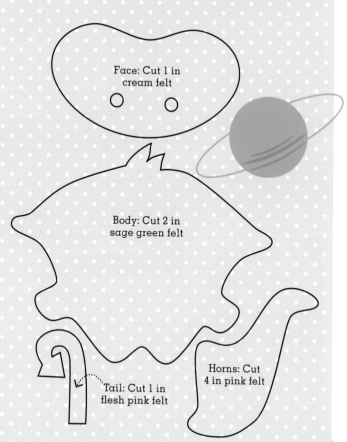

Face: Cut 1 in cream felt

Body: Cut 2 in sage green felt

Tail: Cut 1 in flesh pink felt

Horns: Cut 4 in pink felt

To make *Taurus*

1 Cut out all the felt pieces as marked, either photocopying or scanning the templates, or using tracing paper to make templates, as described on page 4. Use the eyelet pliers to set the two turquoise eyelets in the face piece. Snip out the hoop of the bronze toggle fastening with the metal snips, fold the face in half between the eyelets, and insert the ring through the eyelets. Use the pliers to flatten and close the ring at the back of the felt to make a D shape.

2 Make two small holes in the face with the awl, push a paper fastener through each hole, and open the arms out on the other side of the felt to hold in place. Pin the face piece in position on one of the body pieces, thread an embroidery needle with one strand of cream floss, and stitch in place with a small overhand stitch.

3 Take two of the horn pieces and lay three stripes of organza ribbon across each, pinning them in place, then turning the ends to the back of the felt and gluing them down.

4 Sew the ribbon-striped horns on the front of the face, using an embroidery needle, one strand of pink floss, and a small overhand stitch. Use rubber cement to glue the tail on the front of the body, wrapping the end around to the back of the felt and gluing in place.

5 Glue the other two horn pieces in place on the second body piece.

6 Thread an embroidery needle with one strand of pink floss and then sew the horns together with a small overhand stitch. Stuff the horns through the open, unstitched body with wisps of the stuffing.

7 Thread an embroidery needle with one strand of sage green thread and sew the body pieces together, starting with a small running stitch between the horns (leaving the little crest unstitched) and then completing one side and around the legs. Leave the other side open and stuff the body with wisps of the stuffing, using a matchstick or tweezers to help you. When the body is evenly padded, sew the gap closed.

8 Thread an embroidery needle with two strands of pink floss and sew the flower-shaped mother-of-pearl button onto the right-hand side of the head, positioning it rakishly just above the eye. Rethread the needle with two strands of cream floss and sew four little lines on the hooves, checking the photograph of the finished feltie to get the positioning right.

May 22–June 21 • Ruled by *Mercury* • Colors *Yellow, white, & blue* • Gemstone *Agate*

Gemini the Twins

DIFFICULTY RATING
✳ ✳ ✳

Trying to be everywhere at once is the Twins' way—chat, flirt, charm, maybe a little dexterous pickpocketing, then move on. This sign has good and bad sides, so accentuate the positive, double your ingredients, and pin these two down quickly before they drift away.

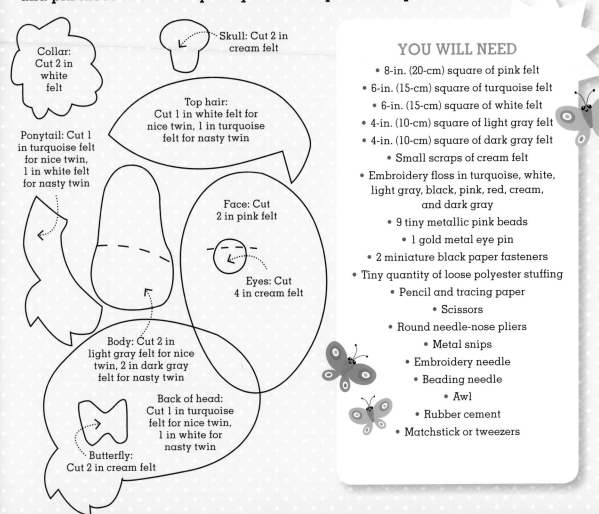

Collar: Cut 2 in white felt

Skull: Cut 2 in cream felt

Top hair: Cut 1 in white felt for nice twin, 1 in turquoise felt for nasty twin

Ponytail: Cut 1 in turquoise felt for nice twin, 1 in white felt for nasty twin

Face: Cut 2 in pink felt

Eyes: Cut 4 in cream felt

Body: Cut 2 in light gray felt for nice twin, 2 in dark gray felt for nasty twin

Back of head: Cut 1 in turquoise felt for nice twin, 1 in white for nasty twin

Butterfly: Cut 2 in cream felt

YOU WILL NEED

- 8-in. (20-cm) square of pink felt
- 6-in. (15-cm) square of turquoise felt
- 6-in. (15-cm) square of white felt
- 4-in. (10-cm) square of light gray felt
- 4-in. (10-cm) square of dark gray felt
- Small scraps of cream felt
- Embroidery floss in turquoise, white, light gray, black, pink, red, cream, and dark gray
- 9 tiny metallic pink beads
- 1 gold metal eye pin
- 2 miniature black paper fasteners
- Tiny quantity of loose polyester stuffing
- Pencil and tracing paper
- Scissors
- Round needle-nose pliers
- Metal snips
- Embroidery needle
- Beading needle
- Awl
- Rubber cement
- Matchstick or tweezers

To make *Gemini*

1 Cut out all the felt pieces as marked, either photocopying or scanning the templates, or using tracing paper to make templates, as described on page 4. Thread an embroidery needle with one strand of turquoise floss and sew the turquoise ponytail onto one pink face (for the nice twin) and the turquoise top hair onto the other pink face (for the nasty twin) with a small overhand stitch.

2 Rethread the needle with one strand of white floss and sew the white top hair onto the nice twin's face and the white ponytail onto the nasty twin's face with a small overhand stitch.

3 Cut the tops off the cream circles for the nasty twin's eyes, as indicated on the pattern (the nice twin's eye circles should be uncut). Use rubber cement to glue the eyes of both twins in place on their faces.

4 Thread an embroidery needle with two strands of light gray floss and embroider the closed eyelids on all the eye circles, using four stitches shaped in a curve for each. Rethread the

needle with two strands of black floss and embroider the eyebrows of both twins, using the satin stitch. Refer to the photograph of the finished figures to follow the shape—the nice twin's eyebrows are small, triangular peaks; the nasty twin's brows are small, down-slanting rectangles.

5 Thread a beading needle with two strands of pink floss and sew the metallic pink beads onto the faces—five on the nasty twin's face and four on the nice twin's—check the photograph of the figures for their position around the brows.

6 Thread an embroidery needle with two strands of red floss and sew the mouths. Both are made from two straight stitches in a V shape—the nasty twin's mouth is an upside-down V, and the nice twin's mouth is an upright V.

7 Align the nice twin's face with the turquoise back-of-head piece, thread an embroidery needle with one strand of white floss, and sew the two head pieces together around the white hair areas with a small overhand stitch. Change to one strand of turquoise floss to sew around the turquoise ponytail piece, and finally to pink floss to sew around the pink lower face area, leaving a gap at the neck. Stuff the head through the neck gap with small wisps of the stuffing, and when it is evenly padded, sew closed. Repeat with the nasty twin's face and head, matching the floss to the colors on the front of the head in the same way. Stuff and sew closed.

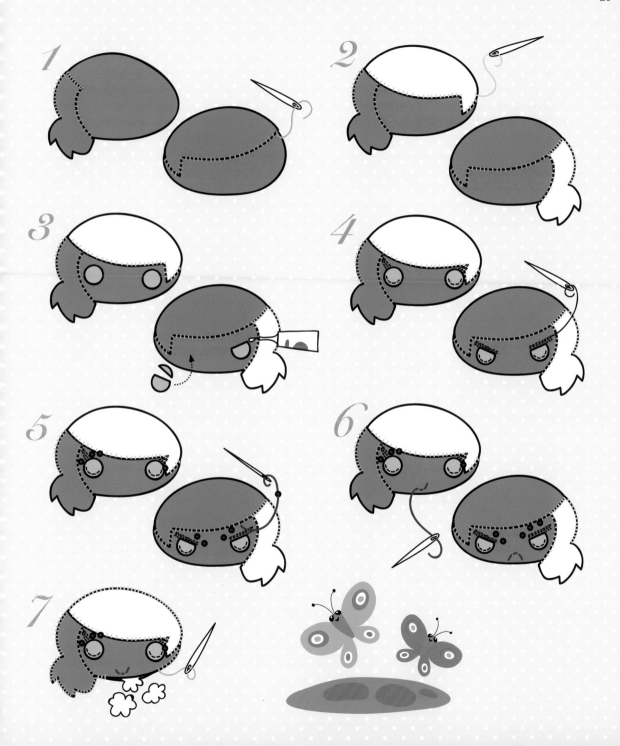

8 Thread an embroidery needle with two strands of turquoise floss and sew a line across the bottom of the nice twin's ponytail. Repeat for nasty twin's ponytail, using white floss.

9 Uncurl the loop in the eye pin and fold it ¹/₄ in. (5 mm) below the loop, then make another loop with the pliers and snip off the rest (this makes the nice twin's butterfly antennae). Sandwich the shaped wire between the two pieces to make the butterfly's wings, and use rubber cement to glue them together. Thread an embroidery needle with two strands of cream floss and sew over and around the wire "body" through both layers of felt to make the butterfly's body.

10 Using an awl, make two tiny holes through one of the skull pieces that will make up the nasty twin's head ornament. Push a miniature black paper fastener through each hole, cut the arms of the fasteners slightly shorter with metal snips, and open them out on the back of the skull. Thread an embroidery needle with two strands of black floss and create the skull's nostrils with two tiny straight stitches, and the skull's mouth with three straight stitches.

11 Spread both skull pieces with a thin layer of rubber cement, wait for a few moments, then align the skull pieces and press together.

12 Sew the butterfly on the nice twin's ponytail, using an embroidery needle threaded with two strands of cream floss. Sew the skull in place on the nasty twin's ponytail.

13 Align the two pale gray body pieces and sew them together, using one strand of pale gray floss and a small overhand stitch. Leave the top open, stuff the body with wisps of the stuffing, using a matchstick or tweezers to help you, then sew the gap closed. Repeat with the dark gray body pieces, using dark gray floss.

14 Thread an embroidery needle with two strands of black floss. Sew a curving line of backstitches on the dark gray body to make a waist, then make a two-strand "tie" by sewing two long parallel stitches, starting at the top of the body and finishing with two French knots just below the waistline. Use rubber cement to adhere one of the white collar pieces at the top of the body.

15 Thread an embroidery needle with two strands of white floss. Sew a waistline of curving backstitches on the light gray body. Use rubber cement to glue the second collar piece at the top of the body, then tie two strands of black floss in a tiny bow and sew it on at the middle point of the collar about ¹/₄ in. (5 mm) from the edge.

16 Thread a needle with two strands of light gray floss and sew the light gray body at the back of the nice twin's head with a small overhand stitch, sewing through the collar and the back of the head to attach it firmly. Rethread the needle with two strands of dark gray thread and repeat the process with the dark gray body and the nasty twin's head.

Cancer the Crab

DIFFICULTY RATING

Clatter, clatter—that's the sound of Cancer rattling her big claws. The crab is the worrier of the zodiac. To make her, consult a moon calendar for the most auspicious time and load every little stitch and every pearly ornament with feeling. Your reward? She'll freely let you use her as a stress doll!

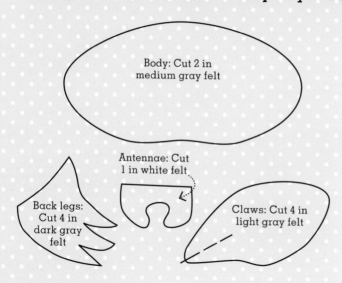

Body: Cut 2 in medium gray felt

Antennae: Cut 1 in white felt

Back legs: Cut 4 in dark gray felt

Claws: Cut 4 in light gray felt

YOU WILL NEED

- 4-in. (10-cm) square of medium gray felt
- 4-in. (10-cm) square of light gray felt
- 3-in. (7.5-cm) square of dark gray felt
- Small scrap of white felt
- Embroidery floss in dark gray, light gray, black, white, and medium gray
- 2 iridescent sequins, ¼ in. (6 mm) diameter
- 2 iridescent sequins, ³⁄₁₆ in. (5 mm) diameter
- 2 white cupped sequins, ⁵⁄₁₆ in. (8 mm) diameter
- 2 orange oval beads, ¼ in. (6 mm) long
- 10 tiny pearl beads
- Tiny quantity of loose polyester stuffing
- Pencil and tracing paper
- Nonpermanent fabric marker
- Scissors
- Embroidery needle
- Beading needle
- Rubber cement
- Awl
- Matchstick or tweezers

To make *Cancer*

1 Cut out all the felt pieces as marked, either photocopying or scanning the templates, or using tracing paper to make templates, as described on page 4. Thread an embroidery needle with two strands of dark gray floss and sew a line of backstitches down the middle of two of the claw pieces, as shown. Rethread the needle with one strand of light gray floss and sew on the iridescent sequins, one large and one small on each claw.

2 Thread an embroidery needle with one strand of light gray floss, align one embroidered and one plain claw piece, and sew them together. Leave the lower end open and stuff with wisps of the stuffing, using a matchstick or tweezers to help you, then sew the gap closed. Repeat to make the second claw.

3 Align the sets of back legs in two pairs, spread one side of each piece with rubber cement, wait for a few moments, then adhere the pairs together. Thread an embroidery needle with two strands of black floss and sew two lines on each set of legs, as shown. Spread a layer of rubber cement on one side of the legs and antenna pieces and on one of the body pieces, then press together.

4 Embroider the mouth and the eyelashes on the second body piece. Thread an embroidery needle with two strands of black floss and make the mouth with three straight stitches in a shallow U shape, and the peaked eyelashes with small areas of satin stitch.

5 Using the point of the awl, pierce two small holes in each white sequin, one on each side. Thread a beading needle with two strands of white floss, thread it through to the front of the body where you want the eye to be placed, then through one hole of one white sequin, through one of the oval orange beads, back through the hole on the other side of the sequin, and finally back through the felt. Knot the thread securely at the back. Repeat for the second eye.

6 Align both the body pieces and sew them together using an embroidery needle, one strand of medium gray floss, and a small overhand stitch. Leave a gap open at the bottom of the head, stuff with wisps of the stuffing, using a matchstick or tweezers to help you, then sew the gap closed.

7 Thread a beading needle with a strand of medium gray floss and sew a row of five tiny pearl beads along the top of the head just below one of the back leg pieces. You will get the neatest finish by sewing the beads on one by one, then passing the needle back through the center of all five in one long stitch to align them. Finish off the thread, then repeat on the other side of the head.

8 Thread an embroidery needle with one strand of light gray floss, place one claw in the right position in front of the body, then sew the body to the back of the claw, using a small overhand stitch. Make one or two tiny stitches behind the top of the claw to hold it in place close to the body.

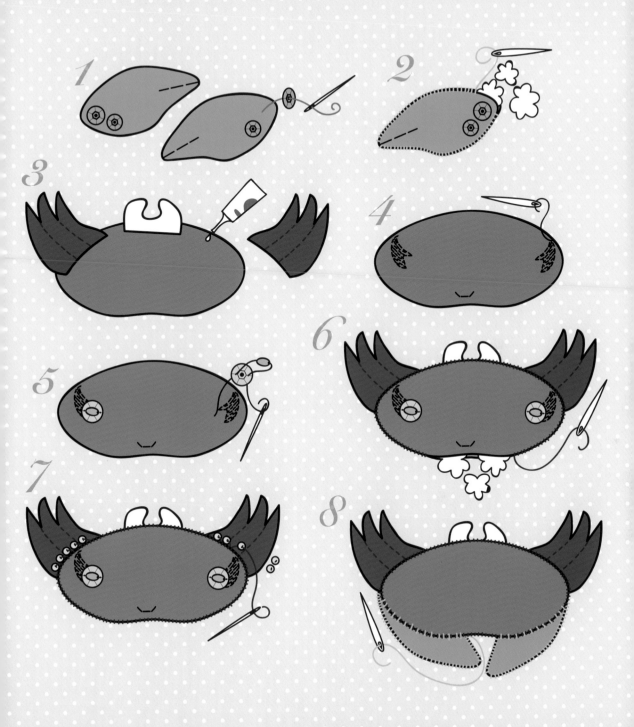

Rules *Cancer* • Associated goddesses *Artemis/Diana, Hecate, Selene, Luna, & Isis* • How big? *Quarter of the size of Earth*

The *Moon*

DIFFICULTY RATING

Don't be fooled by the dreamy innocence of her adorable little face. The moon represents our inner unconscious life, and her changing shape is a metaphor for mood swings. Sew and glue gently—you want this one to stay securely in the land of nod.

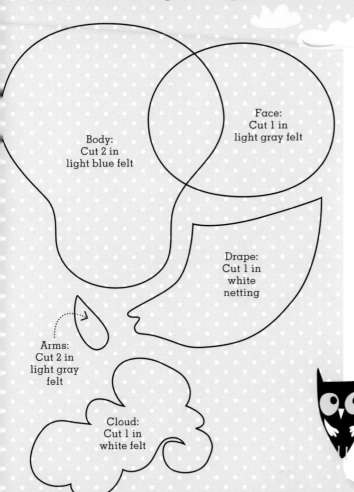

Body:
Cut 2 in
light blue felt

Face:
Cut 1 in
light gray felt

Drape:
Cut 1 in
white
netting

Arms:
Cut 2 in
light gray
felt

Cloud:
Cut 1 in
white felt

YOU WILL NEED

- 6-in. (15-cm) square of light blue felt
- 2-in. (5-cm) square of light gray felt
- 2-in. (5-cm) square of white felt
- 3-in. (7.5-cm) square of white netting
- Embroidery floss in gray, dark gray, white, black, and light blue
- 2 white sequins, ¼ in. (6 mm) diameter
- 2 iridescent cupped sequins, ⅜ in. (10 mm) diameter
- 2 miniature white paper fasteners
- 2 iridescent cupped sequins, 5⁄16 in. (8 mm) diameter
- 4 iridescent cupped sequins, ¼ in. (6 mm) diameter
- 6 crystal seed beads
- Tiny quantity of loose polyester stuffing
- Pencil and tracing paper
- Scissors
- Rubber cement
- Embroidery needle
- Beading needle
- Awl
- Nonpermanent fabric marker
- Matchstick or tweezers

To make the *Moon*

1 Cut out all the felt pieces and the netting piece as marked, either photocopying or scanning the templates, or using tracing paper to make templates, as described on page 4. Spread a thin layer of rubber cement on one of the body pieces, where the arms will go, and another thin layer on the back of the arms. Wait for a few moments, then press the arms in place on the body.

2 Use a thin line of rubber cement to glue the top edge of the netting in place on the body, positioning it so that the face piece will cover the raw edge of the netting.

3 Use rubber cement to glue the face piece in position on the body. Thread an embroidery needle with one strand of gray floss and sew around the edge of the face with a small overhand stitch.

4 Use the awl to make two tiny holes through the face at the point where the sequins for the cheeks will go. Place a white sequin on top of one of the largest iridescent sequins and push the stem of one of the miniature white paper fasteners through both sequins and then through one of the holes. Open out the arms of the fastener behind the face to hold the sequins in place. Repeat on the other side of the face.

5 Draw the line for the hair with the fabric marker. Thread an embroidery needle with two strands of dark gray thread and sew satin stitches to fill in the hair area.

6 Thread an embroidery needle with a single strand of white floss and sew the cloud shape onto the Moon's forehead, using a small overhand stitch. Thread a beading needle with one strand of white floss and sew the remaining six sequins in place on the cloud, using a crystal seed bead to secure each one, as described on page 9. Fasten off the thread after sewing on each sequin and then start again with the next.

7 Thread an embroidery needle with two strands of black floss and make up to four stitches in a gentle curve to create each closed eye. Create the eyelashes with two short stitches at an angle to the eyeline. Rethread the needle with two strands of white thread and sew a curving line down from the brow to make the nose. Make the nostrils by sewing three tiny white stitches in a U shape.

8 Align the front and back body pieces and sew them together, using a single strand of light blue floss and a small overhand stitch, being careful not to catch the cloud when sewing the body pieces together behind it. Leave the bottom open and stuff the body with wisps of the stuffing, using a matchstick or tweezers to help you. When the Moon is evenly filled, sew the gap closed.

Rules *Leo* • Associated gods *Phoebus Apollo, Helios, Ra, Mithras, & Sol* • How big? *109 times larger than Earth*

The *Sun*

Shiny and golden, you couldn't mistake this one for anything but a god. And no wonder—the little sparkler is king of the heavens, however Earth-centric your astrology. Be completely humble as you line up his gleaming bead headdress; you're working with a gilded palette.

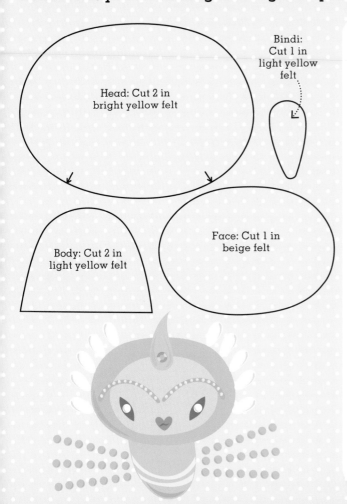

Head: Cut 2 in bright yellow felt

Bindi: Cut 1 in light yellow felt

Body: Cut 2 in light yellow felt

Face: Cut 1 in beige felt

YOU WILL NEED

- 6-in. (15-cm) square of bright yellow felt
- 4-in. (10-cm) square of light yellow felt
- 2-in. (5-cm) square of beige felt
- Embroidery floss in beige, orange, bright yellow, and light yellow
- 2 small, round pearl beads
- 12 yellow seed beads
- 10 light yellow pearl droplet beads
- 11 yellow bugle beads
- 1 small, faceted blue–green bead
- 12-in. (30-cm) length of brass craft wire, 18 AWG (1 mm) thick
- Tiny quantity of loose polyester stuffing
- Pencil and tracing paper
- Nonpermanent fabric marker
- Scissors
- Embroidery needle
- Beading needle
- Round needle-nose pliers
- Superglue
- Rubber cement
- Matchstick or tweezers

To make the *Sun*

1 Cut out all the felt pieces as marked, either photocopying or scanning the templates, or using tracing paper to make templates, as described on page 4. Thread an embroidery needle with a single strand of beige floss and sew the face on one of the head pieces with a small overhand stitch.

2 Thread an embroidery needle with two strands of orange floss and sew small ovals for the eyes, using the satin stitch. Rethread the needle with two strands of beige floss and sew the mouth in a heart shape with small, separate stitches. Thread a beading needle with one strand of orange thread and sew on the pearl beads to make pupils. Rethread the beading needle with a single strand of beige thread and sew on the yellow seed beads above the eyes; use the photograph of the Sun to position them correctly.

3 Cut ten lengths of craft wire, 1¼ in. (3 cm) long. Use the pliers to make a small closed loop at one end of each length. Add a tiny drop of superglue at the other end of each wire and push a droplet bead over the end so that the end of the wire is almost emerging from the top of the bead.

4 Thread an embroidery needle with two strands of bright yellow floss. Sew the wires onto the inside of the second head piece, sewing one on one side, then one on the other. Use several stitches through each loop and along each wire's length, with the stitches sewing through the felt back. Rethread with a single strand of bright yellow floss, align the two head pieces, and sew together using a small overhand stitch, starting at one of the two arrows marked on the pattern piece, up around the beaded wires, and back to the second arrow, fastening off the thread. Stuff the head with wisps of the stuffing, using a matchstick or tweezers to help you.

5 Thread a beading needle with two strands of light yellow floss. Make a small stitch on the lower left-hand side of one body piece, then thread on three bugle beads, pass the beads across to the opposite side of the body, and make a stitch to hold them in place. Repeat, this time adding four beads to the floss, and sewing to hold the beads in place on the opposite side. Bring the needle out between the first two rows, thread on the last four beads, and sew slightly higher on the opposite side, so that the third row crosses over the second.

6 Align the front and back body pieces, thread an embroidery needle with one strand of light yellow floss, and sew together with a small overhand stitch, leaving the neck open. Stuff with wisps of the stuffing, using a matchstick or tweezers.

7 Push the top of the body inside the open neck of the head. Sew in place, using a strand of bright yellow floss and a small overhand stitch.

8 Glue the bindi to the forehead with rubber cement. Thread a beading needle with two strands of light yellow floss and sew on the blue–green bead, knotting the thread at the back.

July 23–August 22 • Ruled by *Sun* • Element *Fire* • Color *Gold* • Gemstone *Ruby*

Leo the Lion

Pile on the rich colors and the confident demeanor. What do you mean it's only a feltie? Lions love the best: luxury, adoration, and an audience, so don't skimp on the materials, and display your exquisitely finished Leo where everyone can see and admire him.

Ears:
Cut 2 in
cream
felt

Head/Mane:
Cut 2 in bright
orange felt

Slits for ears
(on 1 piece)

Face:
Cut 1 in
cream felt

Body: Cut
2 in deep
yellow felt

YOU WILL NEED

- 6-in. (15-cm) square of bright orange felt
- 3-in. (7.5-cm) square of deep yellow felt
- 2-in. (5-cm) square of cream felt
- Embroidery floss in cream, black, khaki green, metallic silver, orange, and yellow
- 2 white seed beads
- 1 gold flower sequin, ⅝ in. (15 mm) diameter
- 1 silver star-shaped sequin, ⅝ in. (15 mm) diameter
- 8-in. (20-cm) length of gold-colored rounded leather necklace cord
- Tiny quantity of loose polyester stuffing
- Pencil and tracing paper
- Nonpermanent fabric marker
- Scissors
- Orange felt-tip pen
- Rubber cement
- Embroidery needle
- Beading needle
- Matchstick or tweezers

To make *Leo*

1 Cut out all the felt pieces as marked, either photocopying or scanning the templates, or using tracing paper to make templates, as described on page 4. Color in the center of each ear piece with the orange felt-tip pen. Spread a thin layer of rubber cement along the lower ¼ in. (6 mm) of each ear. Wait for a few moments, then fold the outer edges of each into the center and glue down.

2 Cut two small slits in one of the head pieces as shown on the pattern. Slide one ear into each slit and glue the ends down on the other side of the felt. Spread a thin layer of rubber cement on the back of the face piece and another on the head, where the face will be glued down, just under the ears. Wait for a few moments, then press the face down on the head to adhere.

3 Thread an embroidery needle with one strand of cream floss and sew around the face with a small overhand stitch.

4 Thread an embroidery needle with two strands of black floss and sew Leo's nose and mouth. The nose is made from two horizontal straight stitches, and the mouth is a double V shape made from straight stitches—check the photograph of the finished Leo for positioning. Thread a beading needle with two strands of khaki green floss and sew two small ovals for the eyes, using the satin stitch. Sew a white seed bead in the center of each to make the pupils.

5 Thread an embroidery needle with one strand of metallic silver floss and first thread on the flower sequin and then the star sequin. Make a series of five stitches to hold the sequins in place on the mane, one stitch between each pair of the star's points. Add a couple of extra straight stitches radiating from each star point to create a sparkle effect.

6 Cut the length of necklace cord in half, thread an embroidery needle with one strand of orange floss, and sew both lengths at the bottom of the second head piece, holding in place with several stitches. Fold the cord from the middle, so that all four ends are pointing downward, and add another couple of stitches to hold in place.

7 Align the two head pieces, thread an embroidery needle with a single strand of orange floss, and sew together with a small overhand stitch. Leave the bottom of the head open and stuff with wisps of the stuffing, using a matchstick or tweezers to help you. Sew the gap closed, sewing between the beard cords. Trim the beard strands to length with sharp scissors, slightly angling the ends.

8 Align the two body pieces, thread an embroidery needle with one strand of yellow floss, and sew together with a small overhand stitch. Leave a gap at the top, stuff with wisps of the stuffing, using a matchstick or tweezers, then sew the gap closed. Sew the body to the head back.

Virgo the Maiden

An organized approach, extreme care, and tiny stitches are all essential; Virgo loves method and detail. You'll want to make sure your sewing comes up to scratch with this beady-eyed gal.

DIFFICULTY RATING

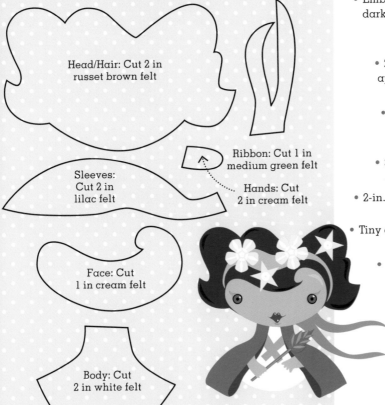

Head/Hair: Cut 2 in russet brown felt

Ribbon: Cut 1 in medium green felt

Sleeves: Cut 2 in lilac felt

Hands: Cut 2 in cream felt

Face: Cut 1 in cream felt

Body: Cut 2 in white felt

YOU WILL NEED

- 6-in. (15-cm) square of russet brown felt
- 2-in. (5-cm) square of cream felt
- 4-in. (10-cm) square of white felt
- 2-in. (5-cm) square of medium green felt
- 4-in. (10-cm) square of lilac felt
- Embroidery floss in beige, mint green, dark red, medium blue, lilac, brown, white, and cream
- 2 blue seed beads
- 2 flower-shaped lilac sequins, approx. ⅝ in. (15 mm) diameter
- 2 lilac cupped sequins
- 2 lilac star-shaped sequins, ⅜ in. (10 mm) diameter
- 4 crystal seed beads
- 3 brown metallic bugle beads
- 1 gold leaf-shaped sequin
- 2-in. (5-cm) length of green felt ribbon, ½ in. (13 mm) wide
- Tiny quantity of loose polyester stuffing
- Pencil and tracing paper
- Nonpermanent fabric marker
- Scissors
- Superglue
- Rubber cement
- Embroidery needle
- Beading needle
- Matchstick or tweezers

To make *Virgo*

1 Cut out all the felt pieces as marked, either photocopying or scanning the templates, or using tracing paper to make templates, as described on page 4. Thread an embroidery needle with a strand of beige floss. Sew the face to the head, using a small overhand stitch.

2 Thread the needle with two strands of green floss and work the headband in satin stitch. Add a few single stitches at each end. For the mouth, rethread with two strands of red floss and sew two horizontal stitches crossed with a V shape. Work a French knot at each top point and sew a stitch at the sides of the mouth. For each eye, rethread with blue floss and sew on a blue bead, hole side up, bringing the thread through the center and back out six times. Extend the eyes with two longer stitches at the edges.

3 Using a beading needle and one strand of lilac floss, sew a flower sequin topped with a round sequin to the headband, securing it with a crystal bead (see page 9). Sew on a star sequin, another flower, and then a star. Glue the felt ribbon to the wrong side of the back head, align the head pieces, and sew together with one strand of brown floss, leaving the bottom open. Stuff with wisps of the stuffing, using a matchstick or tweezers.

4 Thread an embroidery needle with two strands of blue floss. Work a cross in bands of satin stitch, three stitches deep, on one body piece. Rethread the needle with one strand of white thread, align the body pieces, and sew together with a small overhand stitch, leaving a gap at the top. Stuff with wisps of the stuffing, then sew the gap closed.

5 Glue the hands to the sleeves, using rubber cement. Fold the bottom points of the sleeves up so the outer edges align. Thread an embroidery needle with one strand of lilac floss. Using a small overhand stitch, sew the left sleeve to the left body side, from the upper body corner to the neck top, going through both layers of sleeve. Sew back down the sleeve inner edge with small stitches to secure it to the body, and sew behind the hand.

6 Sew through to the back of the body, and use a few stitches to sew the sleeve back to the body edge. Repeat with the right sleeve.

7 Fit the open bottom of the head over the neck of the body. Thread a needle with one strand of cream thread. Sew the head front to the neck with a small overhand stitch. Rethread with one strand of brown floss and sew the head back to the neck.

8 Pass a beading needle threaded with two strands of beige thread, knotted at one end, from the body back through to the lower left of the body front. Thread on the bugle beads and leaf sequin. Pass the needle back through the body at the sequin base, then back to the body front, through the leaf base hole, and back down through all the bugles. Pull the thread tight. Secure the thread between the bugles to the body with single small stitches and fasten neatly on the body back.

September 23–October 22 • Ruled by *Venus* • Element *Air* • Colors *Pink, blue, & green* • Gemstone *Opal*

Libra the Scales

DIFFICULTY RATING
✷ ✷ ✷ ✷

Tough charm characterizes these little scales: Libra demands balance and elegance (in the most delightful yet iron-fisted way). So be extra careful that yours presents a symmetrical face to the world.

YOU WILL NEED

- 6-in. (15-cm) square of bright green felt
- 2½-in. (6-cm) square of white felt
- 2½-in. (6-cm) square of deep pink felt
- Small scrap of white felt
- 3-in. (7.5-cm) square cut from a thick plastic food container (must be flat)
- 5¾-in. (14.5-cm) length of brass craft wire, 18 AWG (1 mm) thick
- Embroidery floss in green, white, pink, black, and dark red
- 2 light green seed beads (try them on the wire to make sure they fit)
- 2 dark amber droplet glass beads (try them on the wire to make sure they fit)
- 2 dark green seed beads (try them on the wire to make sure they fit)
- 1 green star-shaped bead, $\frac{5}{16}$ in. (8 mm)
- 4 clear iridescent flower-shaped sequins, $\frac{5}{8}$ in. (15 mm) diameter
- 4 lilac cupped sequins
- 4 green seed beads
- Tiny quantity of loose polyester stuffing
- Pencil and tracing paper
- Nonpermanent fabric marker
- Scissors
- Fine-tip permanent marker
- Awl
- Round needle-nose pliers
- Embroidery needle and beading needle
- Superglue and rubber cement
- Matchstick or tweezers

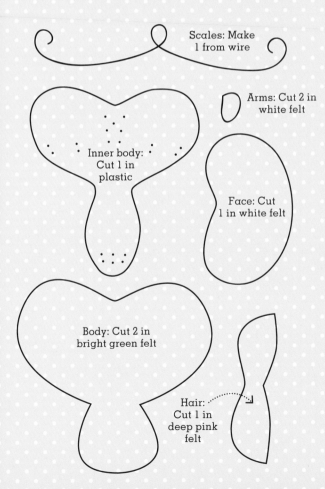

Scales: Make 1 from wire

Arms: Cut 2 in white felt

Inner body: Cut 1 in plastic

Face: Cut 1 in white felt

Body: Cut 2 in bright green felt

Hair: Cut 1 in deep pink felt

To make *Libra*

1   Cut out all the felt pieces as marked, either photocopying or scanning the templates, or using tracing paper to make templates, as described on page 4. Lay the inner body template over the piece of plastic and draw around it with the permanent marker. Use the awl to indent the dots through the pattern into the plastic, then cut the plastic piece out.

2   Push the awl through each dent in the plastic to make small holes.

3   Use the pliers to make a small loop in the middle of the length of craft wire, as shown.

4   Thread first a light green seed bead and then an amber droplet bead onto each end of the wire, then bend the ends of the wire into curves, using the pliers and following the shape shown on the template.

5   Thread an embroidery needle with two strands of green floss and sew the wire onto the plastic inner body piece, using the holes made with the awl. When the scales/earrings are held firmly in place on the plastic, knot and then trim the floss.

6   Place a tiny dab of superglue on the wire on the body side of one of the amber droplet beads and slide the light green seed bead close to the droplet bead to glue it in place. Repeat on the other side. Use dabs of superglue to attach the dark green seed beads on the curled ends of the wire.

7   Spread a thin layer of rubber cement on one side of the face piece and on the head area of one of the body pieces. Wait for a few moments, then press the face in place on the body.

8   Spread a thin layer of rubber cement on one side of the hair piece, and another on the area of the face where it will be glued. Wait for a few moments, then press the hair in place at the top of the face.

9   Thread an embroidery needle with one strand of white floss and sew around the white felt of the face with a small overhand stitch. Rethread with a single strand of pink floss and sew around the hair in the same way.

10   Thread a beading needle with two strands of pink floss and sew the green star bead in the middle of the forehead, at the parting of the hair. Thread an embroidery needle with two strands of black floss and create the closed eyes with gently curved lines of up to four backstitches each, adding little angled stitches to suggest eyelashes.

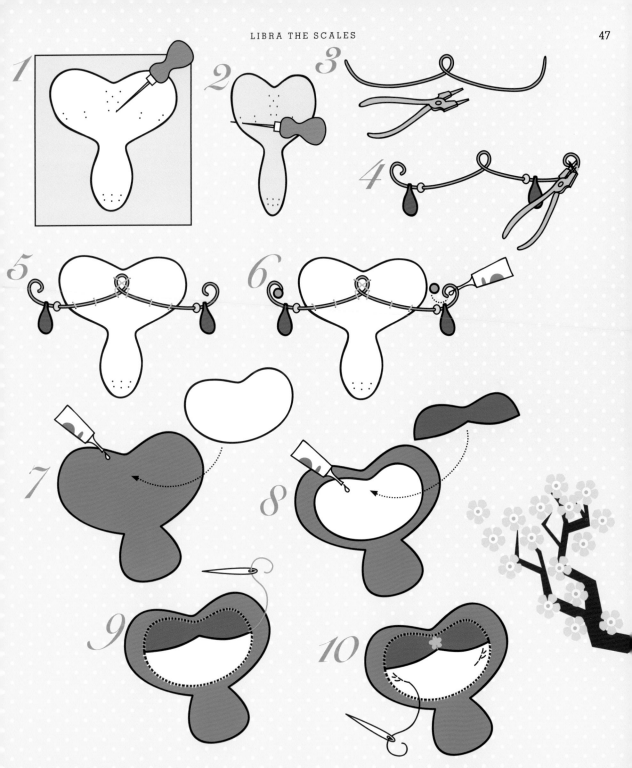

11 Make the nose with two separate straight vertical stitches. Thread an embroidery needle with two strands of dark red floss and make the pouting mouth—first sew a V shape, then a longer single stitch across the top of it. Finish off each of the top points of the V with a French knot to give the mouth extra emphasis.

12 Sandwich the plastic inner body between the two body pieces, letting the scales protrude from each side of the head and the little plastic base stick out at the bottom.

13 Thread an embroidery needle with one strand of green thread. Start to sew around the body at the bottom, sewing through the punched holes in the plastic and continuing around the body's edge, using a small overhand stitch.

14 When you have sewn around half the body and most of the head, stuff Libra with wisps of the stuffing, using a matchstick or tweezers to help you to push the stuffing evenly around the plastic inner piece. When the doll is evenly padded, sew the gap closed.

15 Thread a beading needle with one strand of green floss to sew on the bead and sequin head ornaments. First thread on a clear flower sequin, then a lilac sequin, and finally a green seed bead. Sew in place using the method for securing a sequin with a bead described on page 9, and following the photograph of the finished Libra to place the ornaments correctly.

16 Glue the arms in place by spreading a thin layer of rubber cement on the back of the arms and another layer where they will be positioned on the body, waiting for a few moments, and then pressing in place to secure.

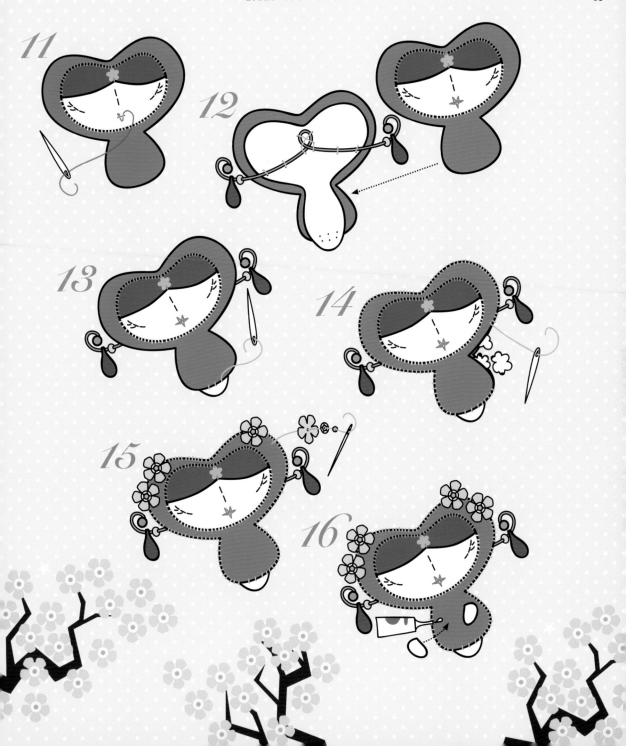

October 23–November 21 • Ruled by *Pluto (& Mars)* • Colors *Black & blood red* • Gemstone *Topaz* • Element *Water*

Scorpio the Scorpion

Even in their cute 'n' teeny feltie form, Scorpions love power and desire. Who would have thought that a scrap of felt could harbor such strong feelings? Don't gaze too deeply into those piercing eyes.

Helmet/Claws:
Cut 2 in dark red felt

Tail: Cut 2 in
light green felt

Face:
Cut 2 in light blue felt

Body:
Cut 2 in turquoise
felt

YOU WILL NEED

- 6-in. (15-cm) square of dark red felt
- 3-in. (7.5-cm) square of light blue felt
- 2-in. (5-cm) square of turquoise felt
- Small scrap of light green felt
- Embroidery floss in turquoise, white, light green, and dark red
- Metallic gold 4-strand embroidery floss
- 2 gold leaf-shaped pendant beads, ⅜ in. (10 mm) long
- 4-in. (10-cm) length of turquoise necklace cord
- Gold jump ring, ⅜ in. (10 mm) diameter
- 2 miniature black paper fasteners
- 2 brown lucite leaf-shaped beads, ⅝ in. (15 mm) long
- 2 pink lucite leaf-shaped beads, ⅝ in. (15 mm) long
- 1 green lucite leaf-shaped bead, ⅝ in. (15 mm) long
- Tiny quantity of loose polyester stuffing
- Pencil and tracing paper
- Scissors
- Rubber cement
- Pins
- Embroidery needle
- Awl
- Beading needle
- Round needle-nose pliers
- Metal snips
- Nonpermanent fabric marker
- Matchstick or tweezers

To make *Scorpio*

1 Cut out all the felt pieces as marked, either photocopying or scanning the templates, or using tracing paper to make templates, as described on page 4. Spread a thin layer of rubber cement on the back of the two face pieces and another layer over the area of the two helmet pieces where they will be stuck, wait for a few moments, then press the face pieces in place.

2 Thread the two gold leaf-shaped beads onto the necklace cord and pin in place on the right side of one of the helmet pieces. Thread an embroidery needle with one strand of turquoise floss and sew the cord in place with single, small overhand stitches. Trim the cord, leaving ½ in. (13 mm) at each end, then turn the ends to the wrong side of the head and sew them down.

3 Use the pliers to open the jump ring and make a small, tight curl in each end. Cut the ring in half with metal snips to make two "eyebrows."

4 Thread an embroidery needle with two strands of white thread and use a small overhand stitch to sew the eyebrows in place. Make two small holes under the eyebrows with the darning needle and push the paper fasteners through them, opening the fastener arms in the back.

5 Thread an embroidery needle with two strands of gold floss and sew two lines of running stitch across the front of one of the body pieces. Thread a beading needle with two strands of turquoise floss and sew the brown and pink leaf-shaped beads in pairs on each side of the second body piece, the brown above the pink. Rethread with two strands of light green floss and sew the green leaf-shaped bead at the lower end of one tail piece. Align the second tail piece over the first, with the bead sandwiched between them, and use rubber cement to glue the two pieces together.

6 Lay the body pieces over the head pieces and mark the overlap with the marker. Spread a thin layer of rubber cement on the inner side of each body piece and the outside of each head piece where the body will overlay, wait for a minute, then glue the body pieces over the head pieces. Glue the tail on the wrong side of the back body piece.

7 Thread an embroidery needle with one strand of turquoise floss, align Scorpio's two sides, sandwiching the tail between them, and use a small overhand stitch to sew them together, sewing between the beads. Stuff the body with wisps of the stuffing, using a matchstick or tweezers to help you. Thread the embroidery needle with one strand of dark red floss and sew around one side of the helmet with a small overhand stitch. Stuff the claw, then sew around the other claw and stuff through the small remaining gap at the top of the head.

8 When Scorpio is firmly padded, sew the gap closed and make a stitch or two around the "stems" of the gold leaf beads so that they are held upright on top of the head.

Rules *Aries* • Associated gods *Mars, Wotan, Tyr, & Mithras* • How big? *Half the size of Earth*

Mars

Mars is the fourth planet from the sun, named for the god of war, action, and other testosterone-fueled activity. Stick the needle in as robustly as you dare just to test how hard he really is.

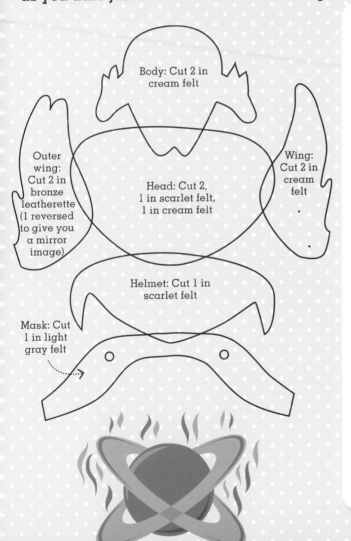

Body: Cut 2 in cream felt

Outer wing: Cut 2 in bronze leatherette (1 reversed to give you a mirror image)

Head: Cut 2, 1 in scarlet felt, 1 in cream felt

Wing: Cut 2 in cream felt

Helmet: Cut 1 in scarlet felt

Mask: Cut 1 in light gray felt

YOU WILL NEED

- 6-in. (15-cm) square of cream felt
- 4-in. x 2-in. (10-cm x 5-cm) piece of light gray felt
- 3¼-in. (8-cm) square of scarlet felt
- 2-in. (5-cm) square of bronze leatherette
- Embroidery floss in light gray, dark gray, bright yellow, scarlet, cream, and bronze
- 2 brass-colored eyelets, ⅛ in. (3 mm) diameter
- 6½-in. (17-cm) length of gold-colored, thin, rounded necklace cord
- Approx. 30 bronzed cupped sequins, ¼ in. (6 mm) diameter
- 1 gold sequin, ⅜ in. (10 mm) diameter
- 1 miniature gold paper fastener
- Tiny quantity of loose polyester stuffing
- Pencil and tracing paper
- Nonpermanent fabric marker
- Scissors
- Eyelet pliers
- Embroidery needle
- Awl
- Rubber cement
- Matchstick or tweezers

To make *Mars*

1 Cut out all the felt and leatherette pieces (apart from the mask), either photocopying or scanning the templates, or using tracing paper to make templates as described on page 4. Draw around the mask on the felt. Use the eyelet pliers to punch two small holes where indicated on the template and set the eyelets. Cut out the mask.

2 Thread an embroidery needle with a strand of light gray floss and sew the mask in place along its top and bottom edges on one of the head pieces with a small overhand stitch. Rethread with two strands of dark gray floss and create the mouth with three straight stitches in an inverted U. Work a tiny angled stitch inside each eyelet.

3 Thread an embroidery needle with one strand of bright yellow floss and sew the helmet in place on the head, working a line of backstitches ⅛ in. (3 mm) in from the helmet edge.

4 Using one strand of bright yellow floss, sew the felt wings on top of the leatherette outer wings, down the outside edge, with small, paired V-shaped stitches. Use the awl to pierce two small holes through the felt only where marked on the pattern. Cut the necklace cord in half and thread one piece in a loop through the holes in each wing. Use one strand of bright yellow floss to make regular stitches over each cord and through the felt and leatherette. Bind the emerging cords with the floss, then finish off and trim the ends. Rubber cement the wings on the back head piece.

5 Align the front and back of the head. Using an embroidery needle, one strand of scarlet floss, and a small overhand stitch, sew around the helmet, then change to one strand of cream floss and sew around half the lower face. Stuff the head with small wisps of the stuffing through the gap, using a matchstick or tweezers. Sew the gap closed.

6 Thread an embroidery needle with one strand of bronze floss. Sew the small bronze sequins onto one body piece in overlapping rows, starting from the bottom and working up. Leave the arms free. Align the body pieces, use rubber cement to glue the arms together; thread a needle with one strand of cream thread and sew together with a small overhand stitch, leaving a gap at the top. Stuff with wisps of the stuffing, using a matchstick or tweezers, then sew the gap closed.

7 Place the head over the body and sew the body to the head with a single strand of cream floss and a small overhand stitch. Cut three 10-in. (25-cm) lengths of bright yellow floss, knot together at one end, and braid to a length of 2½ in. (6 cm). Knot and trim the other end. Sew one end of the braid at the center of Mars's back with an embroidery needle and one strand of bright yellow floss. Bring the braid over the shoulder to the front and push the fastener through the larger gold sequin and the braid, then open the arms on the braid back.

8 Tie the loose end of the braid to the back of the figure.

Venus

DIFFICULTY RATING
✸ ✸

She's the goddess of love, beauty, and fertility. The planet named for her is the second from the Sun, and considered to be a sister to Earth (and you know what sisters can be like.) Make her just as beautiful as felt and beads can be, otherwise there may be trouble.

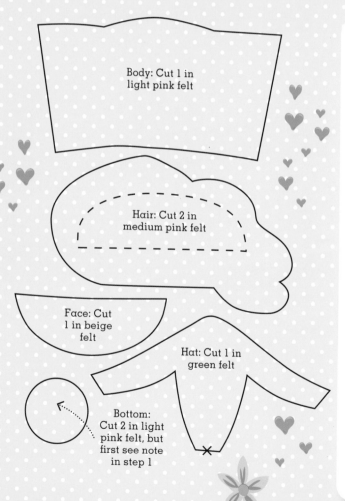

Body: Cut 1 in light pink felt

Hair: Cut 2 in medium pink felt

Face: Cut 1 in beige felt

Hat: Cut 1 in green felt

Bottom: Cut 2 in light pink felt, but first see note in step 1

YOU WILL NEED

- 6-in. (15-cm) square of medium pink felt
- 4-in. (10-cm) square of light pink felt
- 4-in. (10-cm) square of green felt
- 2-in. (5-cm) square of beige felt
- Embroidery floss in light pink, beige, dark red, turquoise, medium pink, and green
- 2 iridescent maple leaf-shaped sequins, 1 in. (25 mm) diameter
- 1 lucite flower bead, ¼ in. (6 mm) diameter
- 1 white round bead, ⅛ in. (3 mm) diameter
- 1 lucite flower bead, ¾ in. (20 mm) diameter
- 1 turquoise round bead, ⅛ in. (3 mm) diameter
- Small quantity of dry rice
- Tiny quantity of loose polyester stuffing
- Pencil and tracing paper
- Nonpermanent fabric marker
- Scissors
- Rubber cement
- Embroidery needle
- Beading needle
- Matchstick or tweezers

To make *Venus*

1 Cut out all the felt pieces as marked, either photocopying or scanning the templates, or using tracing paper to make templates, as described on page 4. Make the bottom of the body from a double layer of felt. Glue together two small pieces of felt with rubber cement, then cut out the shape.

2 Thread an embroidery needle with two strands of light pink floss. Sew the body piece into a tube, using a baseball stitch, then rethread the needle with a one strand of the floss and sew the body bottom into the tube, fitting it in neatly and securing with a small overhand stitch.

3 Fill the body halfway with dry rice, then pack it with small wisps of the stuffing. Thread an embroidery needle with a strand of light pink floss and, using a small overhand stitch, sew the body top closed, with the seam down the center back.

4 Trim one side from one leaf sequin to create a short, flat edge, then thread a beading needle with two strands of light pink floss and sew in place on the body front, making the stitch right through the body. First thread on the smaller flower bead and then the white bead and sew in place over the sequin, as described on page 9.

5 Thread an embroidery needle with one strand of beige floss and sew the face in place on one of the hair pieces with a small overhand stitch. Rethread with two strands of dark red floss and sew the bangs detail in a large running stitch. Make the mouth in satin stitch in a small heart shape. Rethread with two strands of turquoise floss and sew two curving lines of up to four backstitches each for eyes. Rethread with two strands of beige floss to make the curvy line of backstitch for the ponytail detail. Rethread the needle with one strand of medium pink floss, align the two hair pieces, and sew together with a small overhand stitch, leaving the bottom of the face open.

6 Stuff the head with wisps of the stuffing, using a matchstick or tweezers. Push the open neck over the body top, thread an embroidery needle with one strand of beige floss, and sew the face to the body front with a small overhand stitch. Rethread with one strand of medium pink floss and sew the hair back to the body back.

7 Fold the right "arm" of the hat piece up and over. Using a beading needle threaded with one strand of green floss, sew to the central arm. Repeat with the left arm, then turn the hat upside down and pinch the point where the arms are joined together, sewing the corners to the point marked X. Push the needle back through to the front, thread on the other sequin, flower, and turquoise bead, and sew to the hat, as described on page 9.

8 Thread an embroidery needle with a strand of green floss and sew the hat in place, first to the front of the head, around its sides, with a small overhand stitch, then attaching with two small stitches on each side at the head back.

November 22–December 21 • Ruled by *Jupiter* • Element *Fire* • Color *Purple* • Gemstone *Turquoise*

Sagittarius the Archer

DIFFICULTY RATING

The archer is a rough, outdoors kind of feltie, never happier than when he's firing arrows out in the wide-open spaces. Sew neatly for yourself—he won't be impressed with exquisitely tiny threadwork when he could be free, finished, and out galloping across the night sky.

Back of head:
Cut 1 in lavender felt

Body:
Cut 2 in brown felt

Hair: Cut 1 in lavender felt

Face:
Cut 1 in light green felt

Tail: Cut 1 in gray felt

Eye patches: Cut 2 in black felt

YOU WILL NEED

- 4-in. (10-cm) square of lavender felt
- 3-in. (7.5-cm) square of brown felt
- 1-in. x 2-in. (2.5-cm x 5-cm) piece of light green felt
- Small scrap of black felt
- Embroidery floss in yellow, white, bronze, lilac, lavender, and light green
- 3-in. (7.5-cm) length of yellow ribbon, ⅜ in. (10 mm) wide
- 18 lilac seed beads
- 1 embossed 5-pointed silver star sequin
- 2 embroidery needles (for arrow shafts)
- Tiny quantity of loose polyester stuffing
- Pencil and tracing paper
- Nonpermanent fabric marker
- Scissors
- Embroidery needle (to sew with)
- Beading needle
- Rubber cement
- Superglue
- Matchstick or tweezers

To make *Sagittarius*

1 Cut out all the felt pieces as marked, either photocopying or scanning the templates, or using tracing paper to make templates, as described on page 4. Thread an embroidery needle with one strand of yellow floss and sew the ribbon across the face with a line of running stitches at each edge. Trim the ends of the ribbon near the sides of the face.

2 Use rubber cement to glue on the eye patches. Thread an embroidery needle with two strands of white floss and sew the white pupils with small areas of satin stitch. Rethread the needle with two strands of bronze floss and sew two angled stitches, with two more facing them, to make the nostrils.

3 Thread an embroidery needle with a strand of lilac floss and sew the hair piece onto the face with a small overhand stitch, overlapping the left eye, as shown. Thread a beading needle with one strand of lilac floss and sew on the seed beads in a wavy line. Check their position in the photograph of the finished Archer—they are more widely spaced at the far end of the hair.

4 Thread an embroidery needle with one strand of lilac floss and sew together the front and the back head pieces with a small overhand stitch, starting from the point indicated by the arrow in the illustration. Leave the right side of the hair open and stuff the whole lavender hair area, from the side to the floating end, with small wisps of the stuffing, using a matchstick or tweezers to help you. Sew the rest of the hair closed, leaving the green face piece open.

5 Cut a 3¼-in. (8-cm) length of white floss (use all six strands) and sew it around the neck of one body piece, using an embroidery needle threaded with one strand of white floss and making small stitches across it at even intervals. Bring the lower end around the body back and sew it in place (leave the upper end loose, because it will be covered when the face is sewn to the body).

6 Glue the tail on the wrong side of the body, then spread the wrong sides of both body pieces with a thin layer of rubber cement, wait for a few moments, and align and press together.

7 Trim two points from the star sequin to make arrowheads. Lay them convex side down, dab superglue onto the heads of the two embroidery needles, and glue on the arrowheads. Let them dry.

8 Sew the head back to the body back with one strand of lavender floss, using a small overhand stitch. Turn the feltie right way up and push wisps of the stuffing into the face to pad it evenly. Thread an embroidery needle with one strand of light green floss and sew the face to the body front with a small overhand stitch, covering the loose end of the white floss collar. Push the arrows into the body at the right shoulder. Secure at the body edge with a tiny dab of superglue.

December 22–January 20 • Ruled by *Saturn* • Element *Earth* • Colors *Black, gray, & dark green* • Gemstone *Black onyx*

Capricorn the Goat

Save the receipts for sewing materials, says your provident goat feltie—you may be able to offset them against tax. Don't indulge in too many fancy details on this little cutie: Goats like to keep things strictly traditional and within budget.

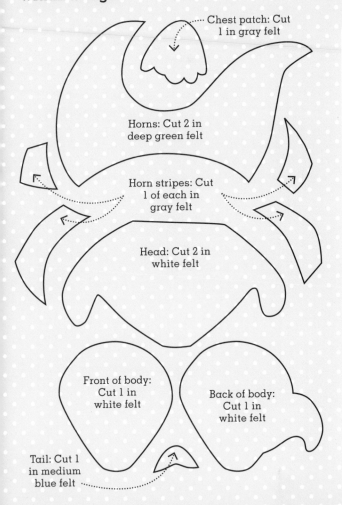

Chest patch: Cut 1 in gray felt

Horns: Cut 2 in deep green felt

Horn stripes: Cut 1 of each in gray felt

Head: Cut 2 in white felt

Front of body: Cut 1 in white felt

Back of body: Cut 1 in white felt

Tail: Cut 1 in medium blue felt

YOU WILL NEED

- 4-in. (10-cm) square of white felt
- 4-in. (10-cm) square of deep green felt
- 2-in. (5-cm) square of gray felt
- Small scrap of medium blue felt
- Embroidery floss in white, gray, and deep green
- 2 black short (half-length) bugle beads
- 3 white bugle beads
- 1 tiny silver sequin
- Approx. 13 silver sequins
- Tiny quantity of loose polyester stuffing
- Pencil and tracing paper
- Nonpermanent fabric marker
- Scissors
- Rubber cement
- Superglue
- Beading needle
- Embroidery needle
- Matchstick or tweezers

To make *Capricorn*

1 Cut out all the felt pieces as marked, either photocopying or scanning the templates, or using tracing paper to make templates, as described on page 4. Spread a thin layer of rubber cement on the back of the four horn stripes and on the corresponding areas on one horn piece (first lay down the stripes to check placement). Wait for a minute, then press the stripes onto the horn piece.

2 Thread a beading needle with two strands of white floss and sew on the two black bugle beads for the eyes. Thread an embroidery needle with two strands of gray floss and make two small angled stitches for each nostril. Rethread the needle with just one strand of gray floss and sew a line of running stitches down the center of the face, between the nostrils.

3 Thread an embroidery needle with one strand of white floss, lay the head piece over the horn piece, making an overlap of ¼ in. (5 mm), and sew the face on with a small overhand stitch. Repeat with the back head and back horn pieces.

4 Thread a beading needle with two strands of white floss and thread on one white bugle bead, then thread the needle around and between the two strands of floss as shown. Sew in the center of the chin on the inside of the back head, making a couple of stitches around the top to hold it firm. Repeat with the other two bugles, one on each side. Add small dabs of superglue over the thread to hold the beads firmly in place.

5 Thread an embroidery needle with a strand of white floss and sew around the bottom of the face and around the ears with a small overhand stitch. Stuff the ears and face with wisps of the stuffing from the open top of the head, using a matchstick or tweezers to help you. Rethread with one strand of deep green floss and sew together the horns along their edges with a blanket stitch. When you have sewn around the first horn, stuff with wisps of the stuffing, then partly sew and stuff the second before sewing the last gap closed.

6 Glue the chest piece to the center of the front body piece. Thread an embroidery needle with two strands of gray floss and sew a T shape to make the division of the front legs.

7 Thread a beading needle with one strand of gray floss and, starting with the tiny sequin at the tail end, sew on all the silver sequins on the back body piece, working in overlapping rows, each row on top of the previous one, until the tail is covered. Sew on the blue tail tip at the end, on the underside of the tail, under the tiny sequin.

8 Thread an embroidery needle with a strand of white floss, align the front and back body pieces, and sew together with a small overhand stitch, sewing carefully between the sequins where the body meets the tail. Leave the top open and fill with wisps of the stuffing, using a matchstick or tweezers. Sew the gap closed. Sew the body to the head back, fastening off the thread neatly.

January 21–February 19 • Ruled by *Uranus (& Saturn)* • Color *Electric blue* • Gemstone *Garnet* • Element *Air*

Aquarius the Water Carrier

DIFFICULTY RATING ✴ ✴

This is one cool feltie, and will be happiest, when fully sewn, to spend his time attached to your laptop, tablet, or cell phone—the Water Carrier has a definite technical bent. Pay particular attention when crafting his magnificent whirlpool of hair, because Aquarius just hates being part of the crowd—this little fella likes to stand out.

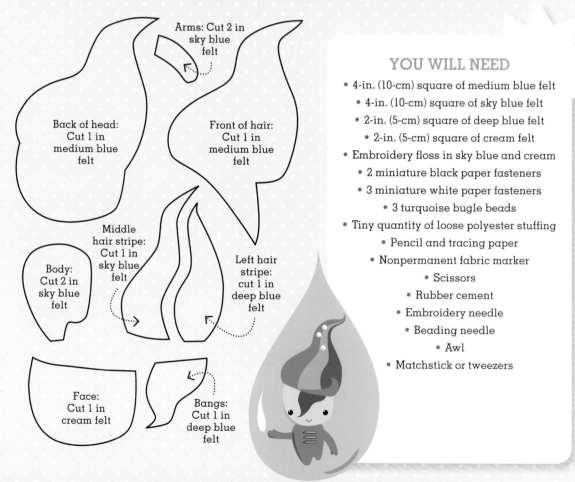

Arms: Cut 2 in sky blue felt

Back of head: Cut 1 in medium blue felt

Front of hair: Cut 1 in medium blue felt

Middle hair stripe: Cut 1 in sky blue felt

Body: Cut 2 in sky blue felt

Left hair stripe: cut 1 in deep blue felt

Face: Cut 1 in cream felt

Bangs: Cut 1 in deep blue felt

YOU WILL NEED

- 4-in. (10-cm) square of medium blue felt
- 4-in. (10-cm) square of sky blue felt
- 2-in. (5-cm) square of deep blue felt
- 2-in. (5-cm) square of cream felt
- Embroidery floss in sky blue and cream
- 2 miniature black paper fasteners
- 3 miniature white paper fasteners
- 3 turquoise bugle beads
- Tiny quantity of loose polyester stuffing
- Pencil and tracing paper
- Nonpermanent fabric marker
- Scissors
- Rubber cement
- Embroidery needle
- Beading needle
- Awl
- Matchstick or tweezers

To make *Aquarius*

1 Cut out all the felt pieces as marked, either photocopying or scanning the templates, or using tracing paper to make templates as described on page 4. Spread thin layers of rubber cement on the back of the bangs piece and where it will be placed on the head, wait a few moments, then glue the bangs in place. Make the eyes by gently pushing the two black paper fasteners through the face (check the photograph of Aquarius for placement) and opening their arms out on the wrong side of the felt to hold in place. Thread an embroidery needle with two strands of sky blue floss and make the mouth with three small stitches.

2 Thread an embroidery needle with two strands of sky blue floss and sew the deep blue hair stripe onto the left-hand side of the front hair piece with a small overhand stitch, aligning with the outer edge. Align the middle, medium blue stripe with the inner edge of the left-hand stripe, and sew it to the front hair piece along both its edges with a small overhand stitch.

3 Use the awl to make small holes through the felt for the white paper fasteners, checking the photograph of the finished Aquarius for placement. Push the fasteners through the holes and open their arms out on the wrong side of the felt to hold in place. Use two strands of sky blue floss to sew the hair in place at the top of the face.

4 Thread an embroidery needle with one strand of sky blue floss, align the face and hair with the back head piece, and sew the hair to the back head piece, using a small overhand stitch. Rethread the needle with a single strand of cream floss and sew the face to the back head piece, leaving a gap at the bottom of the head. Stuff with wisps of the stuffing, using a matchstick or tweezers to help you, then sew the head closed.

5 Thread a beading needle with two strands of sky blue floss and sew the turquoise bugle beads in place on the front body piece. Knot the thread at the back.

6 Spread a thin layer of rubber cement on the inside of the back body piece and the backs of the arm pieces, wait for a few moments, then glue the arms in place. Align the two body pieces and, using an embroidery needle and one strand of sky blue floss, sew around the body with a small overhand stitch. Leave the neck open and stuff the body with wisps of the stuffing, using a matchstick or tweezers to help you. Sew the body closed.

7 Thread an embroidery needle with one strand of sky blue floss and sew the body to the back of the head with a small overhand stitch.

8 Smear a tiny quantity of rubber cement on the tip of the underside of the bangs and another on the hair, where it will be glued down. Wait for a few moments, curl the tip of the bangs up and round, then glue down in a curl.

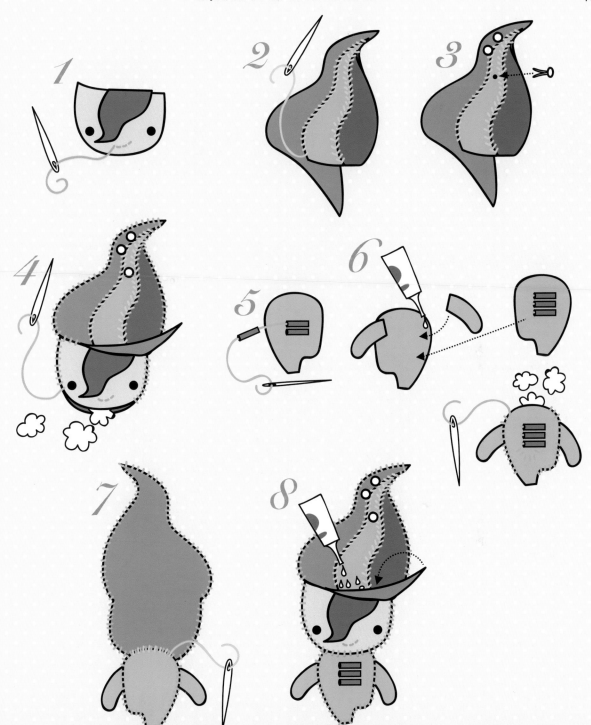

February 20–March 20 • Ruled by *Neptune (& Jupiter)* • Color *Eau de nil* • Gemstone *Amethyst* • Element *Water*

Pisces the Fish

Splish 'n' splash go these shiny charmers as they leap from your craft table. Real-life Pisceans have a slippery tendency to vanish for a day or two, but their feltie versions are more likely to stick around.

YOU WILL NEED

- 6-in. (15-cm) square of light purple felt
- 6-in. (15-cm) square of bright orange felt
- 4-in. (10-cm) square of lilac felt
- 4-in. (10-cm) square of light orange felt
- 2-in. (5-cm) square of black felt
- 2-in. (5-cm) square of fine lilac netting
- Embroidery floss in purple, lilac, orange, and warm yellow
- 2 purple crescent-shaped sequins
- 2 orange crescent-shaped sequins
- 2 pearl droplet beads, 5/16 in. (8 mm) long
- 2 iridescent orange droplet beads, 5/16 in. (8 mm) long
- 6 light pink flat sequins
- 7 bright pink cupped sequins
- 5 lilac cupped sequins
- 7 gold cupped sequins
- 5 copper cupped sequins
- 24 crystal seed beads
- 2 black short bugle beads
- 2 black bugle beads
- Tiny quantity of loose polyester stuffing
- Pencil and tracing paper
- Nonpermanent fabric marker
- Scissors
- Embroidery needle
- Beading needle
- Rubber cement
- Matchstick or tweezers

Bodies: Cut 4, 2 in light purple felt, 2 in bright orange felt

Tails: Cut 2, 1 in lilac felt, 1 in light orange felt

Eyes: Cut 4 in black felt

Heads: Cut 4, 2 in lilac felt, 2 in light orange felt

Nets on tails: Cut 2 in fine lilac netting

To make *Pisces*

Start with the purple fish, then simply repeat the steps with the second set of the materials to make the orange one.

1 Cut out all the felt pieces as marked for both fish, either photocopying or scanning the templates, or using tracing paper to make templates, as described on page 4. Take one purple body piece and one lilac head piece and arrange them so that the body overlaps the head by ¼ in. (5 mm). Using an embroidery needle threaded with one strand of purple floss, sew the body in place on the head, using a small overhand stitch. To make a mirror-image back for the purple fish, reverse the other body and the other head pieces, overlap, and sew together.

2 Place the netting over the lilac tail piece and put the right-facing, front body piece so that it overlaps the tail and the net. Use a strand of purple floss to sew the body onto the sandwiched tail and netting, using a small overhand stitch.

3 Turn the back body piece over so that the wrong side is facing upward. Thread an embroidery needle with one strand of purple floss and sew on the purple crescent-shaped sequins end on, using only one of the sewing holes, so that they serve as fins.

4 Spread a thin layer of rubber cement on both the back of the eyes and where they will be positioned on the front body piece, referring to the photograph of the finished Pisces to position them correctly. Wait for a few moments, then press the eyes in place. Thread a beading needle with one strand of purple floss and sew the pearl droplet beads in place on the eye pieces for pupils.

5 Sew the sequins on the front side of the fish's body. Check the photograph of the finished feltie carefully to place correctly, noting where two are sewn on top of one another. Secure each sequin with a crystal seed bead, as described on page 9.

6 Align the front and back pieces and, using an embroidery needle threaded with one strand of lilac floss, sew together the head end, using a small overhand stitch. When you have sewn around the head, rethread with a strand of purple floss and sew around the body in the same way. Leave a gap at the body top, but don't fasten off the thread.

7 Stuff the fish through the gap in the body with small wisps of the stuffing, using a matchstick or tweezers to help you. When the fish is evenly padded, sew the gap closed.

8 Thread a beading needle with two strands of lilac floss and sew on a short and a long bugle bead to make the mouth. The shorter one should be at the edge of the face, the longer aligned behind it. Sew through all the face layers and knot the thread neatly at the head back. Now make your purple fish's twin, the orange fish.

A Home for Your *Zodiac Felties*

Whether you prefer to keep your little zodiac mascot or if you want to mail it off to a new home, it's good to have somewhere where it will be safe and sound. This spinning-planet background makes a great card to present a feltie, or a neat habitat if you want to perch one on a desk or shelf.

1 Either cut the page along the dotted line or scan the image and print it out.

2 Using a glue stick, glue the background onto a piece of medium-weight cardstock. Smooth it down carefully. (If you want a folded-style greetings card, double the size of the cardstock and glue the background down on one half before folding it.)

3 You can cut slots to mount your feltie or felties onto the card (measure your doll carefully before cutting so that you don't make the slot too big or too small). Alternatively, use small double-sided adhesive tape pads (available online or from any craft store) to hold your feltie in place in the heavens.

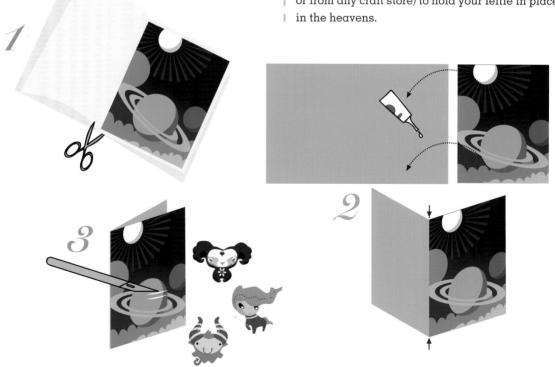

Index